HOW TO CURE
SCHIZOPHRENIA
YES CURE

MARIN PAUN

Paperback: 978-1-958381-73-1
eBook: 978-1-958381-74-8
Library of Congress Control Number: 2022923373

This is a work of nonfiction.

SWEETSPIRE LITERATURE
——— MANAGEMENT ———

Dedication

I would like to dedicate this book to all those people who take their life in the battle with Schizophrenia those are 25 000 people in Australia. Also, to all the people who have schizophrenia and suffer for so long. Schizophrenia is a temporary condition, not a life time condition.

Table of Contents

CHAPTER I

Introduction

T he days when we used to lock up people with mental conditions and forget about them are long gone. These days most of the conditions can be managed if not cured. Why am I talkin g about mental conditions? Because schizophrenia is a mental condition. For the moment it is managed but it can also be cured as I will show you in the book. It is believed that approximately 1 in every 100 people have schizophrenia. It is not known why that is. It is believed that there are certain factors which influence and cause schizophrenia.

Genetics The disease is somewhat hereditary. This is the belief currently held by health professionals. It has to be triggered by an event such as stressful situations, viral infections etc.

Chemistry People with the condition do not have the right balance of chemicals in the brain. Chemicals such a serotonin and dopamine. These chemicals pass messages between different nerve cells contained in the brain.

Illness. Immune deficiencies can increase the likelihood of contracting the disease, actually a mental health condition, because it is not a disease. I will tell you a story which is relevant to this book. Years ago, I used to be friend with a master in eastern philosophy. He had his own group which he belonged to. They were vegetarians, and objects which belonged to individuals were collectively used. You could have borrowed a car or guitar after which someone else in the group will have had access to them. Everything they had, they used to share. I had other things on my mind. Being a vegetarian was the requirement of the group, it was not my cup of tea. I think it takes too much energy and vegetables are more expensive then meat. So I could not join the group even if I wanted. I had my mission being exposed to psychology at the time. The reasons I am telling you this story is because of schizophrenia. He told me (the master) he has a client with schizophrenia. I asked him what it is? What does he do for him? How is it treated? The reason why he has schizophrenia? I said yes that is excellent and I understand. 20 years later while sick in a psychiatric hospital, I found out that schizophrenia is a life time condition. I said what are you talking about? schizophrenia it is a 2-3 year condition. So I am writing this book because I know how to cure schizophrenia, yes cure. Take this book to the health professional and tell him what you know from this book.

Schizophrenia is a temporary condition and is a condition of the mind. It does not have anything to do with the genetics, illness or chemicals in your brain. Is a condition given to you by the mind and not by the brain. The condition is mainly acquired during late teenage or early adolescent years, that is between 18 and 24 years of age. For ladies late 20's and there are some cases in later years. It is believed that if spotted and treated early would be easier to manage. This is not true. If you spot the condition early, the mind is the same as if at later stages. You only treat the symptoms not the cause and this is what the trick is.

There are positive psychotic symptoms and negative psychotic symptoms. The positive ones do not only appear in schizophrenia but in Psychosis, Depression, Alzheimer, Delirium and Bi-polar (manic-depressive). Positive are behaviour plus something. Negative are opposite to positive and is behaviour minus something. It is like you loss something, loss of daily activities, social interaction etc.

Hallucinations

Hallucinations are a disorder in perceptions. They can appear in all five senses seeing, hearing, feeling, smelling and tasting, In the beginning the person with hallucinations does not know the difference between perceptions and himself. The realization of hallucinations come later. Hallucinations can be mood congruent (in harmony with mood) or incongruent (in disharmony with mood).

Tactile. Feeling something that is not there

Olfactory hallucinations. Smelling something which is not there. Substances in general

Gustatory hallucinations are tasting something that is not there. These are less common then other hallucinations and mostly appearing with depression in schizophrenia.

Visual hallucinations are seeing something that is not there. These can be singular light, flashes, shadows and colours, like in the use of LSD. It can be plural deformed faces complex scenes. This is more typical of the delirium.

Auditory hallucinations. Hearing something that is not there. When people with auditory hallucinations are put on a brain scan machine, we see a certain area of the brain lighting up like they do for a real sound. This is normal. When a person is hearing voices, he can tell the difference between the voices in his head and other voices coming out of the speakers for example. Hallucinated voices can come out from the speakers, the TV, from the Radio, own body, other people, animals etc. Sometimes a word is said and some other times phrases full conversation. When the voices are in the second person, for example talking to you they are ordering you to kill yourself.

Delusions

Delusion is a disorder in the thought. Patients who suffer from delusions do not have insight into their illness. They also do not want to be treated. They think they are Messiah future world leaders and other things that are wrong. Delusions can be in mood harmony or not in mood harmony. The delusions change according to your mood like in bi-polar. When you are high you feel the whole world is yours. When you are down you think you are the fault of everything. Mood incongruent delusions are independent from your mood. This is often of the paranoid type. Frequent delusions are:

Somatic delusions (like abdominal organs are decomposing).

Delusions of poverty

Nihilistic delusions (I do not exist anymore)

Delusions of guilt This usually harmonises with the mood. Rises together with depressive Episodes. Unfounded feelings of remorse or guilt at delusional intensity.

Paranoia Someone is after you to get you.

Grandiosity One is omnipotent powerful and grandiose. These can also be featured in episodes of manic depression at the manic stage. 'I am the chosen one'.

Delusions of reference. A message for me in the TV commercial.

Bizarre delusions. As the term suggests they are bizarre delusions like something that could not happened. being cloned by aliens. Delusions are positive and negative, which means perceiving reality plus more or less.

Five important symptoms of schizophrenia.

1. Positive symptoms
2. Negative symptoms
3. Affective symptoms
4. Aggressive symptoms
5. Cognitive symptoms

As I previously mentioned schizophrenia is found in early adulthood for gentleman and late 20's for ladies.

1. As I mentioned before positive symptoms are behaviour plus something, example delusion are positive
2. Negative symptoms is behaviour minus something. All psychological conditions like anxiety depression are negative symptoms.
3. Affective symptoms. Feeling of emptiness and a lot of other depressive symptoms, people often commit suicide, extreme suicide like throwing themselves of a building and any other extreme suicide.
4. Aggressive symptoms are for those who do not understand the world e.g.: I have a solution of changing the world but they do not let me. There is no insight into their own illness. And often they are declared mentally incompetent.
5. Cognitive symptoms. The thinking is affected also in content (delusions) and also in its structure. One thing which I want

to mention is that schizophrenia does not affect intelligence. There are plenty of intelligent people with schizophrenia. The problem here is in attention, concentration and memory. For example, my past memory is not so good and sometimes the current memory too. There are a lot of reasons for that. I live in the present and the past does not concern me. Also because I am doing something else, my mind is on something else. People with cognitive symptoms use made up words. As I said it affects the thinking structure as well e.g.:' the mouse fights the moon in the policeman'. Thinking can be divided without reasons. There is a disorder in comprehension of language. They do not get the 'If" structure. Everything is taken literarily.

Types of schizophrenia

1. Paranoid
2. Disorganised type
3. Catatonic e.g.: Sitting down without expression. Assuming a position without expression.
4. Undifferentiated
5. Residual type

The above system of schizophrenia is used in USA and is called DSM-5.

1. Paranoid type-hallucinations and delusions but no thought disorder or disorganized behaviour. They may be delusive in a persecutory and grandiose way, jealous and even religious.
2. Disorganised type has thought disorder. The speech and behaviour are disorganized. Hallucinations and delusions are less pronounced.

3. Catatonic. Maybe immobile or highly active in movement without a purpose or cause.

4. Undifferentiated. This type of schizophrenia has psychotic symptoms and other symptoms like paranoia, catatonic disorder. Disorganised thoughts are not present.

5. Residual type has positive symptoms, but not severe.

The European system ICD-10 has defined two more categories

1. Post schizophrenic It is a depression of the recently recovered schizophrenia customer. It is an after effect of the condition and also some minor symptoms still exist.

2. Simple Schizophrenia. A development in negative symptoms. And there is no history of the psychotic disorder. There has been a pattern of OCD (obsessive and compulsive disorder) which can be found in schizophrenic patients.

Early Diagnosis of Schizophrenia

It is believed and I am not convinced, that early diagnosis of schizophrenia is beneficiary in curing the condition. There is not a test to ensure 100% of diagnosis. The feeling of the person assessed and the experiences he has had and something which bothers them as well. Schizophrenia symptoms have to reach a serious level before they can be detected.

DSM-5 The American system. According to this you need to show, under clinical supervision for a period of one month, symptoms which have been associated to schizophrenia. Also change in behaviour like social withdrawal, disorganized thought or speech. These symptoms must be lasting 6 months. If a patient is seen to undergo these behaviour, he is considered to live with some form of schizophrenia.

Schizo affective disorder, to avoid confusion, is demarcated from schizophrenia. It contains both bipolar symptoms and schizophrenia, but is not schizophrenia.

There is an assessment report made of eight points, to ensure hallucinations and delusions are part of the patient behaviour.

Kurt-Schneider symptoms encompass a small range of hallucinations and delusions (FRS: Schneider 1959). Auditory hallucinations, thought broadcast, thought insertion, thought withdrawal and delusional perceptions. The presence of a single FRS is considered to be sufficient to reach the diagnosis of schizophrenia. This is no longer relevant to the diagnosis of schizophrenia.

European countries use ICD-10 to diagnose schizophrenia. The DSM-5 analysis is used in the USA and other countries. If the disorder has been persisting for more then a month and less then six months the patient is treated for Schizophreniform disorder,

Brief psychotic disorders are those psychological disturbances lasting for less then a month. The patient is treated for schizoaffective disorders. Without hallucinations and delusions schizophrenia is not considered present. It becomes a case of pervasive developmental disorders (delays in socialization and communication skills).

Psychiatric evaluation is done by asking a lot of questions about the patient and the loved ones. It is good to have the knowledge about the mental history of the patient and their family. When there is no evidence that other illness is causing hallucinations, delusions and other disorders, it is finally decided that the patient has schizophrenia.

The effect schizophrenia has on patients;

Withdrawal from the relationships with family and friends.

Their daily life becomes irregular and peculiar.

They turn to drugs and alcohol being weak. Alcohol is the most used drug.

Chances of suicide increases. There are quiet people who do not talk about suicide but they do it. And there are others who talk to family, friends and doctors needing help. 10% of schizophrenics commit suicide which is a high rate.

Psychotic episodes can last days, weeks and even months. They come frequently and more during stressful times. Important moments in life losing a job, getting married, divorcing loosing a parent. You can not become psychotic because you loose a partner. If you have schizophrenia and you get dumped by your partner then you will have a psychotic attack, but you do not get schizophrenia all of a sudden. The patient has to accept schizophrenia and this is a very long mourning process.

There is a belief which is totally wrong that if you have schizophrenia there is 10% chance that siblings can have it too. This belief is false. It is also believed that environmental factors such hormones, psychosocial life, use of drugs can also have an influence on schizophrenia. If you ask people with schizophrenia they will say that they suffer more from negative symptoms. The psychotic episodes are fun to ride.

Medical Case of Schizophrenia

Second generation medication are to be subscribed because they have lesser side effects then first generation.

Aripiprozale (Abilify)

Asenopine (suphris)

Brex piprozale (rexulti)

Cariprazine (vraylor)

Clozapine (clozonil, versacloz)

Haperidone (Funapt)

Lurasidone (Latude)

Olanzopine (Zyprexa)

Paliperidone (Invega)

Quetiapine (Seroquel)

Risperidone (Risperdal)

Ziprasidone (Geodon)

First generation are:

Chlorpromazine

Fluphenazine

Haloperidol

Perphenazine

The first generation are cheaper and also has more side effects then the second generation. So a balance of drugs should be made. Some anti psychotics can be given by injections in the muscle or underneath the skin. Every two to four weeks depending on the need. They are also helpful when you can not take pills.

Current injections available:

Aripiprozale

Fluphenazine decanoate

Haloperidol decanoate

Risperidone (Risperdal Consta, Perseris)

Paliperidon (Invega Sustena, Invega Trinza)

The treatment you use will be for a while. You do not have to have it all your life. You can even skip it if you can handle psychotic attacks, delusions and hallucinations,

Electroconvulsive therapy or shock treatment is used for adults who do not respond tomedication. Also known as ECT, it can be used for depression. As this condition is for the mind I do not recommend it. It also has side effects of memory loss.

Schizophrenia, how to cure it.

Until now people with schizophrenia were achieving a balanced system in order to live their lives. What does this mean? It means that when you have psychotic episodes, you will recognize that, it is given by the mind (or the brain as it is known) and they will pass. Do not attach them to you, you are here, psychotic episodes come and go,

For some reasons, functional reasons, there is not a perfect world. Like flying in a balloon around the world, even if you have not achieved your mission you might die and lose your life. As I previously mentioned the mind is working on two equal area fragments instead of one. What we need to do is to build a bigger fragment that will take over from the two and the schizophrenia will disappear. No more delusions and no more hallucinations. We can do that by meditating for 2 to 3 years for 2 hours a day. If you are below 50 years of age you will also acquire self esteem and be more have more do more and also fulfill yourself by achieving your mission. The steps required for this change are given in this book. It will follow schizophrenia and will give a strong basis for more books to follow. So, schizophrenia is a condition of the mind and is not at security issue but a functionality problem, not as the psychiatrist will tell you and like you to believe.

All I am saying is that you go to the health professional with this book and show to him/her the cure.

Psychosis, Schizophrenia, Split Personality Disorder.

Psychosis is a condition which is found by itself as psychosis, but also in the mind of schizophrenia. It includes hallucinations and delusions. They are sometimes paralysing and you do not do much. You want to withdraw from activities such as socialising, work and others. Hallucinations and delusions can affect someone to act in a bizarre way. If you display the symptoms of psychosis, it means you can suffer from a lot of mental conditions. A schizophrenic can have psychotic symptoms but a psychotic can not have schizophrenia. Psychosis can occur at any age in time unlike schizophrenia in early 20's and sometimes in adult life. Psychosis following a recovery can be experienced again. I am not an expert in psychosis but I have done my research. Psychosis can be brought on by a stressful situation and emotional and physical series of events. An example of psychoses are: post natal depression following the birth of a child. Also post-traumatic stress syndrome where the person can not see the reality and pictures of an event over and over again. A definition of psychosis would be: Inability of accepting the facts as they are and manufactures others to suit their own facts. It is possibly easy to experience psychosis. Also, the diagnosis requires more substance. During a life time people will experience an episode of psychosis. Removing the stress factor and time can result in full recovery.

Psychosis and schizophrenia

Psychosis can be the result of a range of medical issues like dementia (includes Alzheimer), neurological problems (including Parkinson's),

HIV, strokes and even some form of epilepsy. Psychosis is believed to be related to brain function, in particular dopamine and neurotransmission changes. It allows cell to communicate with each other. A high level of dopamine suggest the ability to communicate between cells is reduced. It appears to be directly responsible for incidents in psychosis. It also affects the memory, socially acceptance and behaviours are altered. High level of dopamine will affect your self awareness. The grey matter in people with psychosis seems to be reduced, so this affects the ability of thought as a normal person. The above change in brain function is temporary. However in people who have schizophrenia it is a longer in time. The understanding of psychosis is at a greater level due to research done,

Split Personality and Schizophrenia

It is believed that people who suffer from schizophrenia have a split personality disorder or multiple personality disorder. Many schizophrenics suffer from voices in their head which seem to be real, and they talk to them and it can appear that they have multiple personality disorders. This is not true. Each personality is a fragment. The brain has fragments or a variety of other personalities. But there is only one person. With multiple personality disorder there are a variety of symptoms known as Dissociative Identity Disorder. Many symptoms are similar to schizophrenia.

Depression this is not always present in schizophrenia but with personality disorder this is regular.

Anxiety is common for a lot of mental diseases. It is part of everybody's life and is hard to distinguish between acceptable levels and high levels. When schizophrenics are told that their delusions are not real they get anxious.

Suicide 10% of people with schizophrenia commit suicide. This is because they can not deal with hallucinations, they become part of them. As a previously mentioned it is imperative to detach from hallucinations and seeing delusions as part of the mind not you. Hallucinations come and go. People with personality disorder try to take their life too. The voices in their head do not allow just a universal voice as a person should have. And it becomes depressive and they commit suicide.

Substance Abuse. It is believed that people with schizophrenia are open to substance abuse such as drugs and alcohol. You can not deal with the situation at hand and find an escape in addictions. If you use substances you will become addicted. It is normal 95% of people are addicted. Someone with multiple personality disorder as well can turn to drug and alcohol and become addicted.

Obsessive and compulsive disorder Is not found in schizophrenic maybe a bit in catatonic schizophrenia. It is believed that these symptoms develope with multiple personality disorders as a coping mechanism by giving some degree of control in life.

Hallucinations Both states multiple personality disorders and schizophrenia are affected by the inability of the brain to see the difference between reality and fantasy. Those with multiple personality have it to a lesser degree.It is one of the basic conditions of schizophrenia.

Sleep issues As you wrestle with delusions and hallucinations you will begin to experience sleep issues. People with multiple personality disorder, because of their continuous voice hearing are likely to be prone to sleeping problems. There is always someone to talk to all night.

Mood swings A Theses are part of multiple personality disorder because they are mental health issues. The same for schizophrenia it is a mental condition. It should be but it is not. It is only found in people with schizoaffective disorders.

Eating disorders This is not found in people with schizophrenia. It is found in multi personality conditions. But it is not a condition by itself as it might be so diagnosed. It is part of the condition,

Mood Swings B Dramatic mood swings are unique to bi-polar and not to multiple personality disorders or schizophrenic. I am talking about long moods and not the one when you are happy a minute and unhappy the other. Because you can become withdrawn in social activities, bi-polar is confused with schizophrenia. It is easy to confuse the two conditions because one crosses the other. There is medication for people with bi-polar and they can lead to a normal life. Also, medication is prescribed because it takes out fluctuations in the mood. With the right psychological support you can integrate multiple elements in to one personality. Each of the personality is part of their identity. They do not have delusions and hallucinations. Because of the closeness in symptoms it is difficult and doctors should be cautious when making a diagnosis. Harmful treatment methods can be used.

Help one with schizophrenia by being supportive, understanding and loving.

For everybody it is good to have a friend, a friend who will be there for you anytime you want or need him or her. Caring, understanding, sensitive and loving. More true for a person who is diagnosed with schizophrenia. That you know what is getting through, how he feels, how he behaves and you can see his point of view.

At times dealing with a person who has schizophrenia might be challenging and hard. You need to realize that you are not the only help.

There are health professionals, community workers, people at church, and support groups who will help you. You do not have to take the whole burden. Also a degree of responsibility for the condition has to be assigned to the person who has the condition. You will need to accept the condition. People get sick, whether mentally or physically. 95% of people get sick, it is not our fault. But we need to raise to the challenge past the condition and live as full a life as possible. There is going to be a lot of feelings of frustration, fear, guilt, embarrassment, helplessness, emotions which we need to deal with it.

It is not a life time condition it is a passing temporary condition and eventually you will recover. Look at the end of the journey, where you will see the patient cured. And as I said it can happen to everybody not only you. You might see the patient suffer and you do not want that. But this is temporary it will pass. A very powerful command in cognitive therapy is 'it will pass'. It is not you, you are here. The delusion in schizophrenic is given by the mind and it will pass.

Any mental disorder has a stigma attached to it and so has schizophrenia. It is believed that everybody (he/she) needs to deal with it. There is no perfect person in terms of mental conditions.

You will loose respect and reputation because you have a person sick with schizophrenia. You can say that you live in an insensitive world, cold world. Instead of getting help you are getting the ridiculous. So, every time you hear people ridicule you it is about them being not sensitive enough.

Do not take the situation hard, be light on yourself and see the funny side. The expectations of curing the condition is around 2 to 3 years. It is not going to be any faster, it takes this time to cure. You will get through low times when the condition will be at its worst. Make the patient feel confident and competent. Enjoy your day and do not forget about you. Just because you are supporting a patient it does not mean, that you neglect yourself. Look after your health. You will need to be loved and feel important. You will also need your own care, somebody to look after you in the same way you look after your patient. As I mentioned everybody needs a friend. You have your own needs. Find people who have a common goal as you. People who will understand you. Maybe you will need a support group, for people with schizophrenia or people who have been through schizophrenia. It is not a life-time condition where you live under a balanced system recognizing the schizophrenia and moving along with life. People with schizophrenia are the best because they know what to do in case of immediate help.

Fill up your life with beautiful fulfilling tasks like playing an instrument, reading, painting, gardening, go out, watch movies and any other activity you might think of. Sleeping which is a number one priority needs to be abundant. Get 8 hours sleep and even longer if it is required. Exercise and live healthy. This is a condition takes time so you need to look after yourself. Almost 40% of the population are overweight. If you are one of them just go on a good diet like ketose where you cut down on sugar and starches. It might be difficult to find time to look after yourself. But find friends away from schizophrenia. If you can do that.

In time you might develop some associative negative emotions such as irritable, impatience grumpiness. You will need to deal with these emotions as they might have an impact on your patient. Live your life to the full, taking into account that you live one day at a time, and that there is plenty of time for fun and enjoyment apart from challenges (like schizophrenia).

You are not the cause of the schizophrenia, so do not feel responsible for things which do not go according to plan. It takes time as I said, to cure the condition. There will be times when the patient will not agree with the condition 'imposed on to him', because he is 'perfect'. There is also a stigma but this is best dealt with by making people insensitive to people's problems. It is a cold world.

It is good to take the medication until solved, until the delusions, hallucinations and psychotic attacks will be handled better. The patient needs to stick to the medication. People who have psychotic attacks are hard to convince to take medicines because they are convinced they are right and are saying there is an external threat to their lives. It will be hard to convince the person they are sick. Allow the patient the freedom he wants, let him pick his own doctors, talk about general problems like insomnia, lack of appetite.

Personally myself, I am against medication because they have some terrific side effects such as weight gain, insomnia, libido loss, moving limbs, diabetes, and others. But if the episode is a long one maybe there is a requirement. The patient has to realize that he is not the schizophrenia, that it is given by the mind and it is only temporary condition. You are still here, this is the essence of threating a schizophrenic.

The medication needs to be tested and be adjusted so it finds the right response in you, This will take a while maybe even months, because doctors allow 2 to 4 weeks for testing the medication. If one medication is subscribed and tested properly you need to make sure that she/he takes the medication regularly. There will be relapses, and this will take place because medication has been discontinued. As soon as there is a relapse make sure the medication has been taken.

If the schizophrenia has subdued you feel there is no need for medication. You are wrong that the medication needs not taken. The doctors know more about medication then you or the patient. If you notice relapses, paranoia, delusions, insomnia, withdrawal, it is good to call the doctor straight away, because there is a need for the doctor. There might be a situation in which the patient needs to be taken to the hospital because there is a regress of the situation. Be ready for that and take all the precautions.

The patient needs a good spot to live and sleep. A family with children and grandchildren might not be an ideal situation and alternative places needs to be found. Like health care centers. Also, if the patient is addicted to drugs and alcohol he needs a place to sleep. Home might not be a great environment. The best thing is to talk to doctors about possible accommodation, you can find help also with local community health centers. There are all sorts of options depending on the need of the patient. Opportunities where you can share can be considered, transitional housings where managers take care of you, SRS (supportive recreational services although you need a lot of money), acute hospitals and others. The best for the patient is at home in a positive loving understanding environment.

You need to remember that the experience is empowering for the patient, this is another mental condition which will help you to grow. It is all part of life experiences. It is a temporary condition and it is not the patient, also not you the carer.

People who lived and had schizophrenia.

Also the purpose of this book is not to make you live with schizophrenia for all you life, but there are people who in the past who have lived and worked while having schizophrenia. The research as far is not good for schizophrenia. That is because they do not know the cause.

Some notable names which achieved a balance state and come out victorious are: Dr John Forbes Nash Jr. who was honoured with a Noble Prize for economics, a great mathematician of today who suffered from schizophrenia. He had delusions and hallucinations together with a great mind for economics.

Peter Green the founder of Fleetwood Mac a great guitarist struggled with violent years of schizophrenia and was hospitalised for years. Syd Barrett founder of Pink Floyd is believed to have been suffering from schizophrenia. Jeremy Oxley musician and member of the Australian band Sunnyboys. Brian Wilson former leader of the Beach Boys and Grammy Award winner and singer. Lionel Aldridge helped the Green Bay Packers win two superballs and stayed in NFL for ten glorious years. He retired from football and a few years later developed schizophrenia, struggled for a while but in the end he achieve balance and so lived for long time.

Conclusions

As mental conditions have attached to them a stigma, i.e. people are running away form you syndrome, we like to note that these people are insensitive, and it has nothing to do with you. It is them by being cold in front of the situation. There is also a lot of information across various conditions as information becomes more and more available. I would like to tell you and reiterate that schizophrenia is not a life time condition where you obtain a balance of the system. So, you can live your life. Schizophrenia is a 2 to 3 years condition where you will meditate every day for 2 hours. While doing that, the schizophrenia will recede. You can also use medication where symptoms will not be felt so much. It is best to take this book to the psychiatrist and work together with him and with this new light into schizophrenia. This is the cure for schizophrenia, a non-functional part of the mind.

A confirmed diagnosis of schizophrenia allows someone to get the right kind of help, which includes a good health team.

Assumption that schizophrenics are violent is absurd. Obviously there can be moments of frustration and anger. It takes a while to cure the condition. If someone has a psychotic attack (a psychotic episode), get out all the people and remain only with the patient. Wait until he becomes more patient and then deal with the situation. You did not choose to be schizophrenic but you choose to cure the condition. I do not know too much about the condition and I am not an authority in the subject, but I know what it is. It is a condition of the mind. The previous and the hallucinations and delusions are the only things I knew about schizophrenia. While I have done some research my knowledge of the condition is up to date. I want people who have schizophrenia, chronic fatigue syndrome and addictions to achieve their full potential by achieving their mission. We are all here on earth to do things for others. The more we do the quicker we will change the world. That is why I included in a good part of the book, an insight into psychology. And this is where I want the schizophrenic to go. I wish you luck with the condition and to develop yourself as much as you can. Good luck.

CHAPTER II

Development

Change in the system

If your life does not require changes, in the sense that your system is travelling well and there is no need to change, do not change. The changes in your system might produce an unbalanced system where life might become hard. Live in the moment. By living in the moment I mean live your life one day at a time. There is no future, no past, only the moment. In this world you will find an abundance of two things, everyday moments and relationships. But relationships requires work, work on both sides of the relationship to keep it alive. The eastern philosopher introduces you to the idea of mindful meditation. Specifically where you live your life being aware of your surroundings and yourself which is at the moment. I suggest to let go of the past and let go of the future. You learn from the past and then you let go. It is with the past that you can do nothing but learn and let go. The process of letting go is a powerful tool in personal development. You will see the need to let go and then you let go. You let go from the gut E.g.: 'I let go of a relationship which is finished and it is in the past there is nothing I can do about it'. This can be applied to a lot of situations where you need to let go.

Once you live in the moment

Once you live in the moment you will start living. Living is in the moment because this is the only things abundant. In general people are negative and what they really remember about facts are negatives. They will dwell on a negative situation. If you make a habit of reliving the moments in a day, more than once you will have lots of living moments. This is one thing that you can try and if it works you can keep doing it.

Watch your energies.

You will need energy to rewrite your system, to re-programme yourself. That is why I said you will need energies. Also, to be happy you need to charge the battery at a level of 70%. While you re-programme yourself, you will have more and more energy.

You will need to know where you lose energy, and where you gain energies. While in contact with some people you will lose energy, while in contact with others you will gain energies. Completing tasks will give you energies, not completing them will make you feel deflated and procrastinated.

Sleeping is important, proper sleep will get you energies. Bad sleep will lose energies. When you have a lot of energies it is possible to save them for later. We all have a battery in the subconscious mind where energies are used and stored. Save energy for later, by commanding 'I save energy in the subconscious battery'. Or release it by commanding saying: 'I release energy from my subconscious battery'.

Watching energies is a very important process. I have not watched my energies and ended up with Chronic Fatigue Syndrome, a very hard condition where you only have 12% of the battery capacity.

Make a living.

If you would be an eastern philosopher master in India you would not have the need to make a living, you would be surrounded by people and making a living would not be necessary. But here in the western world you would need to make a living. You will need to provide for yourself and at the same time develop yourself. Do not expect that someone will give you a job. You will need to get a job and build jobs.

It is hard to make a living and I am referring to 'good jobs' which pay well, they are challenging and you get your social skills. If you do not focus on making a living the sheriff will get your furniture and you will end up on streets.

Know yourself.

The reason I put this on the top of priority is because if you do not know yourself you will live in ignorance and confusion. Know what you are doing and why are you doing it. What makes you tick and what do you want from life? These are the type of questions you need to ask yourself. Some authors put knowing yourself at the end of the development. I believe it is very important and you need special time in the beginning, not to live in Ignorance and Confusion.

Assume total responsibility

Assume total responsibility for your life. It is very important to be totally responsible. All your life you can not give total responsibility away. You are in charge of your life, you are the architect of your life. People in general are not doing things for you. So, if you want to progress in your life you need to be totally responsible. You cannot be responsible in one area and not responsible in other areas. Totally responsibility is required. Personally I was not totally responsible, and I needed to start from the beginning everything again. You can not give away responsibility, only control. You need to become responsible yourself and let go of blaming. Blaming everyone for things you need to be responsible, blaming the government, blaming the doctors. Although the government should be responsible they are not and they probably do not care in a majority of cases. So, stop blaming everyone apart from you. And if you blame yourself, you still do not do it, thinking there are no requirements for the action to take place. A good example would be my mum, who grew up in a negative destructive environment. When she does not have anyone else to blame, but herself, she lets go of the action. Blaming looks in the past 'who did it?', Where areas responsibility looks in the future 'what can we do from here?' Being solution oriented rather than problems oriented, is good.

One high goals is the mission.

It is believed that 4000 years ago, due to some proof, a movement to start changing the world started. It was decided that something must be done. In order to change the current world of hurt, world of attack and world of security. Because life was so painful, a movement to change the world was started. Most of the knowledge to change the world was acquired 2000 years ago (not all but most). It does not make any sense to be born, multiply, work and die. There must be something more. And in my opinions we are all here for others. Great lovers such as Jesus of Nazareth, Buddha and Mohamed were born to teach the message of universal love and unite the world. They spoke of a world where everybody is united through love. These are the greatest lovers of our civilization. Others such as Mother Theresa, Albert Schweitzer and Florence Nightingale were also great. You only become great if you lose in a mission better and grander than yourself. I am not asking why greatness but how greatness. By loosing yourself in a mission which is grand, you change the world faster and you are also a role model for other people. 'Built to last' and 'From good to great' by Jim Collins who emphasizes how to look and become great. It is probably put in your soul before you were born. From good to great shows how to become great from good and that good is the enemy of the great, 'Built to last' emphasizes how to build institutions for the next century and well after. Achieving greatness means that you serve with honour the human race and is the reason that your time spent on earth is well worth. Unfortunately only 2-5% of any given generation achieve their mission. If we all fulfilled our missions the world would have been better a long time ago. Significant contributions to change the world faster are to be proliferated. Thinking big, also changes the world faster and in the same time you are more fulfilled, because you have made significant contributions. You do not have to be a psychologist to understand that.

To achieve and know your mission to find out why are you here, is to always ask the question: 'What should it be?', 'What can it be?', 'How should it be?'. My current mission is to achieve significant contribution and make the world a better place. It can be in any area

Peace of Mind why is peace of mind so important,? If you do not have it you will not enjoy life in general. So, it is your duty to keep your mind clear. Your goal is to be free of mind clutter, so you can enjoy life and what you have. It is a very important goal in becoming a happy person. A happy person is who you would like to be. Eliminate all the problems of your mind which do not have any place. A way to peace of mind is to write down on a piece of paper what bothers you on one column and how to let go of them from your gut. As I previously mentioned your letting go is a powerful tool. You will develop a good habit of letting go.

Work with the superconscious mind.

If you do not master the superconscious mind your life would be hard. By going with the flow in the right direction dictated by you, you will make life easier. The superconscious mind is a mind above all the other minds, of which we all have access at any time. All life comes from the superconscious mind. Once you have a superconscious solution it will be simpler and you will think 'Why didn't I think of it.' It will answer all the questions. It will be full of energy and has a feeling of elation. The superconscious mind can be accessed through written goals, affirmations, day dreaming, relaxation etc. When you use the superconscious mind the solution will come and you need to take immediate action, otherwise it thinks you are not serious. So, master the superconscious solution by taking the first step and then follow the steps as they come. Synchronicity is a process of using the superconscious mind, where 3 or more events relate to themselves to bring you a solution. Events which seemed not related to each other are connected in order to bring a solution. Serendipity is the process of making happy discovery on your way to your goal.

The superconscious mind has access to all data making the solution true or false. The more you use the superconscious mind the easier it becomes to use. You can get a lot of energy from the superconscious mind, sometimes running for days without sleep. Personally, I forget to take action in order to start the superconscious solution and by doing that life becomes hard. You can activate the superconscious mind by going in solitude for 30 to 60 minutes. After which a solution will come up full of energy. You will need to take action and follow the steps of the solution.

Acquiring self-esteem.

Self esteem for me is the most important issue in the whole book. It is how much you love yourself, how much you like yourself, how much you accept yourself unconditionally for who you are. With self esteem you can face and do anything, You can face rejection, you can face failure, you can face anything. It is important to acquire self-esteem and to become a generator of self esteem. By the power of suggestion you will have some changes in your self esteem towards the ego. But you will become hungry for self esteem to keep away the ego suggestions. The affirmation area is powerful tool to programme your mind, and we use them to acquire self esteem Affirmations are statements in the present tense, present tense because the subconscious mind only work in the present. Affirmation needs to be emotionalised and aloud for maximum input. They uses the word 'I' which can only be used by you. The subconscious mind does not take the negative 'not' e.g.: 'I am proficient' and 'I am not proficient'. You can replace not with regardless or without.

Because for years we used to 'hate' ourselves, it is hard to change over night into 'love yourself'. We can love ourselves a bit more today than yesterday and a bit more tomorrow than today. Which can be transformed into following affirmations:

'I like myself more today than yesterday
And 'I like myself more tomorrow than today'
'I like myself unconditionally'

Now on top of this affirmation you need to like yourselves in various roles, e.g.: Good father. See yourself as a good father, spend quality time with your child, love your child. I love my son, And you should use any roles you have such as; teacher, employee, husband and so on.

After re-living these roles and using affirmations you will feel the difference in 3 weeks, a month, 3 months, a year and 3 years. To acquire self-esteem it takes on average of 3 to 4 years. After that you will be able to go anywhere, because you love yourself. So, use the following affirmations aloud:

4X I like myself unconditionally

4X I like myself more today than yesterday

4X I like myself more tomorrow than today

4X I am a worthy and valuable human being no matter what I do and say ('or regardless of what I do and say I am still a worthy and valuable human being')

4X I am a worthy and valuable human being no matter what happens

4X I am good enough regardless how I go in any situation

4X I am good enough regardless how I do in any situation

4X I am good enough regardless what people think about me

4X I am good enough regardless what people say about me

4X I am good enough regardless of the people's opinion about me

4X I am good enough because GOD say so. He makes all people worthy and valuable with a mission on earth

4X I am good enough because I am the father of all children

4X I am good enough because I am a good father, I love my child, I do the best thing for my child

4X I am good enough because I still have a relationship with my parents (others throw them in asylums and nursing homes)

4X I am good enough because I am committed to people

4X I am good enough because I am a sensitive person

4X I am good enough because I am a caring person

4X I am good enough because I am a doer and I complete actions

4X I am good enough because I do the best I can with the knowledge at the time

4X I am good enough regardless of my mistakes

4X I am a worthy and valuable human being regardless of my mistakes

Some of the affirmations are long and they become Cognitive thoughts. I am able to remember these affirmations by heart, because I have been doing them for a while. You are better off writing them down on a piece of paper. The subconscious mind is open to suggestions in the morning when you wake up and in the evening before you go to bed. If you are in an environment of 'rejection', I suggest that you repeat the affirmations/ cognitive thoughts so you counter act the negative suggestions. Something else I need to mention is to leave some parts of yourself to the ego, around 20%. That is because it is a world of ego with scoring points and opinions about people. Also, you do not want to be used as a doormat, that is where ego helps. In general, the ego takes the back seat of the car.

You may acquire self-esteem with your own affirmations. Even if you have self esteem is good to repeat the affirmations from time to time because of the power of suggestion from being surrounded by a negative environment.

Fill your own mind with loving thoughts.

On TV you get a lot of crimes and actions in the movies. Shows like news are negative in the sense that they emphasize the negative and not the positive. Wherever you go you will be surrounded by society's negativity. You will need to fill up your mind with spiritual, uplifting, loving, warm and positive thoughts. You can spend like 30 minutes per day of your time to focus on these positive thoughts. If it is not possible do it just once per week.

Learn to forgive

If this is the first personal development book discovered you will probably be upset with your parents, that is because they have not been supportive while you grew up. And you are entitled to be so. After a while you will need to forgive them. They did their best they could with the knowledge from their parents and so on. It is healthy to forgive and let go. Be selfish and let go of the past from the people who did wrong to you. Forgive but don't forget.

Take care of your body.

The body is complicated and can perform a lot of functions in little time. It is known as the mind of the universe because it can do so many things including listening to the universe. It is also the temple of the soul. Take care of your body by giving it good food and good exercise. The diet is more important than exercise, 20% is exercise and 80% is diet. Ideally speaking of diet and books 30% of populations are obese and overweight. Thanks God that there are solutions the for big problems that society has. Gary Taubes in his book 'Why you get fat and what to do about it', covers all the questions pertaining to weight loss. It is based on the research done at the end of 19th century and the beginning of 20th century, research forgotten. It also throws away the false believe we had from the research done at the end of 20th century. It is shown we should not eat to burn sugar and we should eat to burn fat. By burning sugar we create fat. By eliminating most of the starches (even all) and sugars for two weeks we set up the system to burn fat. And then once or twice a week we eat sugars and starches so the hormones leptin and testosterone can grow to eat the fat. You will also get rid of the craving of sugar and starches by cheating twice. They are called cheat meals because you eat them twice a week and you can eat as much as you would like starches and sugars. Meat and vegetables (as much as you want) and a bit of fruit (not too much because they contain fructose which is a sugar). A sugar is still sugar even if is natural. You will be able to stay without food for days. Until the hunt of animals was completed. And the fruits eaten at the time were small with little sugar. If you eat too much fruit you will not lose weight. It seems to me that this diet is the answer to society's problems and not portion control so much used these days, where you end up putting weight back on eating whatever you want.

World of love.

Some people believe that there is a world of dominance. Is it? Some people who love power say there is a world of power. A world where people would push people around. The truth is that the world is a world of love. Derived from the movement in the superconscious of security where we would live to feel safe and secured. Love does that. The truth is the game of dominance, force fear and intimidation is boring. A game where you impose yourself on other people, could be this called living? In order to change the world we need to bring into the world what was meant to be and that is the world of love and after that change it. The jump to a new world as tried by some people is too much to ask. We need first to unite ourselves in love, and after that, change it so there is no hurt. You can be like a flower where energies are flowing through you. You have children so to have loving relationships. You have marriages to have loving relationships. You only need to give a bit of love away so there would be some coming back. The more you give, the more would come back. By following the steps in this book you will become a loving person and a loving person is the one you should become. Just because is simple does not mean it is easy, this requires a lot of effort and the final outcome is worth waiting.

Deal with negative emotions.

When I talk about negative emotions I do not talk about the emotions of loss of a relationship or the passing away of somebody you love. But about negative emotions such as doubt, fear, envy, resentment, guilt which are not warranted, and you spend a lot of time of dwelling on them and that stop you from achieving a happy fulfilled life. Justifications keep the negative emotions alive it cultivates them. You are saying 'I am entitled to this emotion ', or you say 'After so much trouble can I give up?' The idea is to let go of the luggage of negative emotions, get rid of them. Justification keeps the negative emotions alive. By dis-identifying you keep the emotions at bay, they lose control over you. 'I have anger but I am not the anger', 'I have anger but the anger is not me'. You are still here and the emotions will pass. Blaming is at the root of negative emotions. Once you stop blaming so the negative emotions stop. Negative emotions are learned throughout your life. Being judgemental is another way of keeping the negative emotions intact. Where there is a division there is a struggle. Responsibility and freedom go hand in hand. You obtain freedom to the degree to which you are responsible. As I previously mentioned the idea is to leave negative emotions like garbage and go ahead and fulfil your life. The difference between successful and non-successful people is how they deal with negative emotions, so they have time to have a happy fulfilled life.

Lack of childhood love affects the negative emotions. Parents must love themselves and from there, each other and the child.

General Anxiety

The main theme in general anxiety is worries. Apart from that there is always an impending sense of danger, you are not the beneficiary of life.

Everything seems to be danger, the world is a danger, humanity is at danger, life is a danger. When you suffer from anxiety you will always be negative looking for the bad in everything.

Trigger thoughts or precipitating thoughts as called by psychologists are the thoughts before the emotion which triggers the event. They can be found after the event as well and they can be relieved through imagination. In anger example: 'How dare she says that to me.' In case of a relationship a sense of loss 'She does not love me anymore' when the relationship is finished. You need to stop yourself from identifying with your thoughts e.g. 'that is how relationships end'. 'There is nothing I can do to get him.' This is writing more appropriate trigger thoughts. You will need identifying rules which give rise to the trigger thoughts, because if not they will make you to hold on to them. You will need to look at concepts such as: 'guilt', 'anger', 'power', 'religion', 'love', 'uniqueness' etc. You will need to identify the trigger thoughts which rob you of living a fulfilling life. We need to replace them with more appropriate trigger thoughts. The trigger thoughts have a control over us.

After all, we cover so far, in general anxiety and worries are the main theme. I recommend you the course run by The Center for Clinical Studies. Is a very practical course in a sense that there are a lot of exercises and is also free. There is a worry diary where to stressful situations a series of logical questions are applied that thus deal with the worry. It is called the worry diary.

About the worries
What am I worried about? List my worry thoughts?
What am I predicting? How much do I believe it will happen? (0-100%)
What emotions am I feeling? And rate the intension of the emotion (0-100%)

Challenging the worry

What is the evidence for your predictions?

What is the evidence against my prediction?

How likely is it that I am predicting will happen? (0-100%)

What is the worst that could happen?

What is the best that could happen?

What is the mostly thing that will happen?

How helpful is for me to worry about this?

If the worst thing will happen what could I do to cope?

How else can I view the situation?

Balanced thinking

A more balanced and helpful thought to replace my worries is-------

How much do I believe in my predictions? (0-100%)

How intense are my feelings/emotions? (0-100%)

By challenging the worries they will have a less effect on to you to a point where they do not affect you.

Another way to deal with worries is to let go from the gut. E.g. Worried that you are going to fall in the shower even if you have taken all precautions not to fall. The trigger thoughts 'Hi what am I going to do?' I am going to fall. The anxiety that I am going to fall in the shower is not a truth, not a fact, not a reality just an unhelpful thought.

Letting go is like a deviation of energy, you do not stop it, you deviate it. How you need to let go, is practise. The more you are doing it the easier it will come. Do it for three times and the worry will disappear. We also need to practice mindful meditation which is in the present. In the present there is no fear e.g.: I rest my leg on the chair, my fingers touch my body, The corner of the table is there. And so on. Remember that worries are good to plan for the future.

Depression

There are two types of depression, one is reactive depression, where there are links to external events and endogenous which seems to come with no reasons. The reason I cover depression is that there is no reason to live for a lot of people, people try to take their own lives and we can not watch how people suffering.

Depression is a continuous feeling of sadness from which it is hard to escape. In depression there is always a feeling of loss which triggers off the event. In order to deal with depression, we need to identify a feeling of loss and rob it of its powers. It maybe a feeling that we lost a childhood, that we do not have kids, that we wasted our life. In depression you need to identify what you lost and then replace them with more appropriate thoughts to today's life. If you do not have kids, you can sponsor some, there are so many kids without parents in this world. If you did not have a childhood try to live your inner child in the present.

When you wake up in the morning, the depression is at its peak. It is important not to identify with the feelings at this stage. You have a thought but you are not the thought, you have thought but the thought is not you, and you keep it at a distance (the thought comes and goes you are still here). You have a feeling but you are not the feeling, you have a feeling but the feeling is not you (they come and go and you are still here). As previously mentioned, there are trigger thoughts associated with the event. We have trigger thoughts such as;' What is the use of waking up?', 'I can not face the day'. No matter what the thoughts and feelings are you need to get up and start your day.

Start with activities which will preoccupy the mind so to get out of the state of depression. Do not do an activity which does not serve the purpose of putting the mind on something else than depression. Every time you finish a task you will acquire energy and the more tasks you finish, the more energy you will have and that will get you out of depression.

We need to get out of bed to make sure the trigger thoughts of depression do not have time to trigger the depression, and also complete tasks which will energise you. Also seeking out beautiful surroundings, the sun, the nature, the light will ensure that you gradually snap out of the depression. The trigger thought identified has to be replaced by more helpful appropriate thoughts 'It is only the depression, it will pass', 'I do not have energy for anything', 'Slowly and surely I can build my energy'.

The hypnopompic state is a state between sleeping and waking up, as we return to consciousness. It plays an important part in influencing our waking up feelings. Before we go to bed we can say affirmations, positive cognitive thoughts for the morning. E.g.: 'I wake up in the morning feeling good',' I wake up in the morning tomorrow and I feel wonderful'. Do not make the affirmations too long that will confuse the mind. Also do not make it unbelievable: 'I wake up in the morning feeling fantastic'. The mind will not believe it. By dealing with depression you will empower yourself with the future knowledge of getting out of depression. So, depression is not bad it is empowering. There will be definitely other chances of depression which you will know how to deal with. You will need to be patient and ready for setbacks but your perseverance will pay off in the end. As mentioned with trigger thoughts you will need to look at inner rules, regulations and distorted thinking which give rise to trigger thoughts and events. E.g.: Something is lost and there is nothing left of value in people's lives. That life without marriage is not worth living. There are a lot of things to do in your life as opposed to what you cannot do. It is believed that in depression, influenced by it, self-esteem is the culprit. Acquire self esteem by seeing yourself as a worthy and valuable human being unconditionally or for who you are and not for what others think about you. By replacing inner rules, regulation and distorted thinking with more appropriate ones, the trigger thoughts, which give rise to depression will be dropped and replaced by more appropriate ones.

Anxiety attacks.

Like in many forms of anxiety, at the base of anxiety lies fear. Fear is produced by being overwhelmed by actions and tasks. While suffering anxiety attacks, you will have numerous trigger thoughts, more than general anxiety. Some will be hard to stop. When they are not stopped, the adrenalin and fear will eat your body. In this period of time you will lose an enormous amount of body weight. Personally I lost 15 kilos in 3 days, because I could not stop the anxiety attacks. After 3 days of anxiety, the attacks stopped and realised that it was taking place in the spirit and not the mind. Doctor uses Valium to stop anxiety attacks, but sometimes it works and sometimes it does not work. You should not have more than 4 major tasks to work on, and also a small number of activities. If you have more than 4 tasks you will trigger anxiety attacks. If you have less than two you will not be able to work with the superconscious mind and life will be hard. You will always think about the one goal which will block the action from the superconscious mind. To get rid of the actions and tasks you will write them on paper. Actions on the left side and what to do about them on the right side. The letting go technique will come in handy and you know it by now. Let go of what you do not need e.g.:' I let go of building the house'

It can happen that this time the fear entered the gut, and you need to work on your gut. You need to replace trigger thoughts in your spirit. The trigger thoughts in your mind need to be replaced by more appropriate thoughts 'It is only temporary it will pass', 'Hi, what am I going to do? 'Everything is OK I can handle the situation'. Working on the number of tasks and actions you do, combined with trigger thoughts will help you with anxiety attacks. You will need to work on the central theme of anxiety, which is worries.

Panic attacks.

The reason you get panic attacks is because you lack fulfilment in your life. And I do not mean being busy, but meaningful tasks that fill your void in your life. Like relationships, meaningful purpose of life, goals which are important and so on. Panic attacks are anxiety, but in acute form. Trigger thoughts of panic attacks have a sense of urgency 'This is my death warrant','I am going to die','This is it'. I know panic attacks first hand because I used to have them. Panic attacks start in elevators, in overcrowded places, and if you are by yourself in situations you do not like. In the middle of panic attacks your breath is short and you are panting. It is nothing to worry about, you are not going to die.

The trigger thoughts in panic attack need to be replaced by more appropriate and realistic ones. 'This is temporary, it will pass', ' this is the panic attack it will pass'. 'this is OK I can handle the situation'.

The trigger thoughts encountered in panic attacks will produce additional trigger thoughts such as 'I am going to have a heart attack','I am going to die','I am going to wet myself'. Trigger thoughts give rise to more trigger thoughts because of the physical symptoms they produce and so on. The key is not to identify with them, they are temporary, they will pass. You have a thought but the thought is not you. I have a thought, but I am not the thought. There is the mistaken inner view that if something bad can happen, something bad will happen. Such a belief is good in children, but not for a mature individual. If something bad can happen, in most occasions it will not happen. It is temporary, it will pass, is a positive way of looking at the trigger thought.

Paranoia.

Recently I have discovered a patient with paranoia and because of that I will try to make a point about paranoia. Also you might think it is not a hard condition it can really have an effect on you. People will have paranoia so friends and other people will agree with them and give their self esteem a boost. Every time you are right your self esteem goes up. That is the whole mechanism of paranoia. Is also a feeling that everybody is gaining against you. There is strong evidence that the conclusion is not valid, but the person with paranoia will not agree. The trigger thoughts of people with paranoia are: 'They know I am right but they would not admit it', 'It is bloody unfair'. Until we understand why we always need to feel right it is very hard to get rid of paranoia.

Phobias

Phobia is a powerful fear which comes with an element of irrationality. We all have phobias. Some phobias are: fear of heights, fear of enclosed spaces, fear of spiders, fear of dentist (as I used to have), fear of public speaking, fear of dogs and so on. Just because you have a phobia does not mean that you have more anxiety than the general public.

Psychologists call phobias fixation phobias and traumatic phobias. The fixation phobia is the phobia which has not been outgrown (keeps us fixated) and keeps us at the same age. The traumatic phobia is connected with a single traumatic event which we did not understood fully. E.g.: Fear of fire, fear of public peaking, fear of dogs, fear of spiders. Whatever the phobia type is, it spells terrifying threats and has to do with the fear of losing control. The dentist will take control over our mouth and inflict pain. The dog is going to take us by the throat. There are many things over which we do not have control and we do no phobias. We can discuss the treatment with the dentist to give us drugs to anesthetized us. We can use a device which will keep the dog away. And slowly, slowly learn the art of public speaking. Flying is more safe than busses and trains, so the fall of the plane is highly unlikely.

The regulations, inner rules and distorted thinking can be used together with trigger thoughts to deal with phobias. We have nothing to fear from close paces, heights, fear of flying, fear of open spaces etc., provided we take up precautions which are good for everybody else.

Obsessive and compulsive thoughts.

I could not believe that the condition of obsessive and compulsive thoughts could inflict such pain. Until I encountered people suffering and being on medication. As with previous kinds of anxiety, we need to look at the distorted thinking, inner rules and regulations and trigger thoughts and replace them with more appropriate thoughts for today's world and more mature views. As the name suggests the compulsive thoughts are those thoughts which compel us to perform certain unwanted actions and obsessive thoughts are those we see for what they are but refuse to go away. Examples of compulsive thoughts wash our hands even if they are not dirty, check the garage it is locked even if we checked it before. Obsessive thoughts are the thoughts that we have to please 'mummy' and 'daddy'.

If they wash and scrub everything that is associated with dirt, they will be a worthy and valuable human being. The trigger thoughts which accompany the obsessional feeling of cleanliness are: 'It will make me dirty and therefore repulsive', 'I will catch a terrible disease,' 'I should never be able to get clean'.

When obsessive thoughts lead to compulsive ones, the trigger thoughts are possible 'It is the only way to stop the thought'. 'If I can only do that things will be OK' The trigger thoughts can be replaced by 'dirt easily washes off', 'things like that make no difference in life'. The rule is that you are a worthy and valuable human being because of who you are, and you are not worthy because somebody else says so even if it is somebody in authority. We have obsessive and compulsive thoughts to atone for a feeling of not being good enough. This is a rule which needs to be replaced. Another rule is that if you touch everything twice it will make it right or make one happy.

The trigger thoughts :' I will never be forgiven', 'How could I have done such thing', 'I must be a terrible person'. Give rise to the inner rule that you are the only person in the world that could do such things, that nobody will love you and that there is nothing you can do to be a worthy and valuable human being. Where the trigger thought is an obsessional one leading to a compulsive urge to do something dreadful is 'What is the worst possible thing I can do: steal from somebody', 'kill somebody' it destroys all irrational thoughts. The trigger thought is the fear of your own bad imagination put there by an experience which punish 'badness' with feelings of guilt. When you endlessly check things, the trigger thought is 'What is one thing for the moment that will spoil my happiness'. No matter how sure you are, you still check things twice and sometimes do not know how to stop it. You must observe it and will eventually go. Do not be judgemental just observant. Even if you have compulsive and obsessive thoughts you have nothing to regret. You still deserve happiness and success in this life. The suffering of the people with obsessive and compulsive behaviour comes from the wrong interpretation with which these actions have been surrounded.

Conversion disorders and amnesia.

In extreme cases they are rare. I put a chapter on this because I know of people who suffer from amnesia and conversion disorders and I have encountered myself in terms of mind shutting down. Also I lost my hearing which is a conversion disorder.

The trigger thoughts involved in conversion disorders are: 'I can not handle this',' I must blot out everything.' And in a major form of conversion disorder the person collapses (like my mother did). Another trigger thought is: 'If I am sick, people will leave me alone'. This trigger thought is carried on from childhood where you could get away with being sick. No we are not in childhood anymore, when an adult will take care of us when we have too much to handle. We need to apply mature rules and regulations to the current situation. If it is too much, let go of some them, tell yourself that you can handle the situation, and all the physical functions begin to return to normal.

The power of positive thinking.

Thinking has power and is best described by positive thinking. I do not want to omit the negative emotions which are part of us. By focusing on positive you will attract positive and by focusing on negative you will attract negative in your life. By focusing on positive you will be mentally healthy. By having a habit of focusing on negative you will not have good mental health. By negative emotions I mean worry, anxiety, fear, anger which is not related to losing someone or divorcing. Instead of focusing on negatives you will focus on your goals and have no time for the negatives.

Change need to like or want. If you look properly need, the dependency is applied too often in our lives. More appropriate would be to replace them by 'like' and 'want'. There are things we need but not so many as we tell to ourselves. **Change 'awful' to 'inconvenienced'.** Awful means something bad happened. Inconvenient is a word which causes just a bit of nuisance. To deal with awful we use contingency plan, that things are not going to go the way we want to: trains will run late, people will let you down, jobs will take longer. We need to recognize life for what it is, not for what we want it to be. Saying the word awful is also judgemental and keeps the negative emotions alive, something we do not want. **Change 'must' or 'should' to 'could'.** It is important to re-examine values, actions and beliefs, sometimes because they were put in us by some other people. 'Must' and 'should' brings a sense of duty but 'could' brings an element of choice which we need. **Change 'judge' and 'evaluate' to 'observe.'** By being judgemental you keep the negative emotions alive, and by observing them you use the highest form of intelligence assigned to the human race. Evaluating is unavoidable like values. We do not obtain values if you are not evaluating. Reserving judgements until there is more data is a way to behave. **Change 'hurt' to 'teach'.** We have to recognize that we often learn more from the people who want to hurt us, then people who are nice. To allow to be hurt is to allow the person with intent to achieve his purpose. But it also gives us the opportunity to look at ourselves; ready to take offence; unrealistic expectations ; that others will not treat us the way we want to **Change 'embarrass' to 'amuse'.** Embarrassment is a fear that we would be laughed at. As to be seen as a buffoon is not what we want, an incompetent person that is. You would not like your self-imaging to be at the mercy of someone's else. Embarrassment is a fear which enters life around 4 to 5 years. Also the more embarrassed we feel, the more we invite others to laugh. And the more we can laugh at ourselves the less we are going to be laughed at. So change 'embarrass' to 'amuse' and see the joke with everybody else. **Change 'scare' to 'confront'** One way in dealing with fear is to confront the fear. By confronting the fear we see things different and you are not paralysed by fear. Life is not a secure business. By facing the fear we learn from that and we develop our human potential. **Change 'discourage' to 'challenge'**. Discouraged means doing things has gone out of you. A way of dealing with discourage is to change it to 'challenge'. Challenge is uplifting and generates its own energy. Challenge is something you rise to.

More about the power of thinking and the power of words.

People who have a psychological problem use words such as: 'awful', 'bad', 'hurt', 'embarrass', etc. They also use evaluation and judgement in their daily life. Life is seen as intimidating, overwhelming and dangerous and have a vocabulary of incompetence and failure. You can compare these messages about yourself with messages sent by someone who sends deprecating comments all the time. You will feel inadequate, a failure, low in confidence that you do not amount to much. **About the power of words** If we want to change psychologically we need to use the right words. Words have power and you begin to recognize this by covering this book. Words are symbols which represent reality. The power of suggestion for example when you say to yourself that you are stupid a lot of times, you will believe you are stupid

If you believe that you are worthy and valuable, and you tell that to yourself numerous times you believe you are worthy. The verb 'to be' or 'I am', is the verb which helps us in viewing the power of words. 'I am tired', 'I am depressed', 'I am worried', 'I am helpless'. They represent me temporarily and not me permanently. A more appropriate word would be; 'I feel depressed', 'I feel sad', 'I feel helpless' .Other areas to consider in the power of words are the adjectives. E.g.: 'stupid', 'idiot'. Use adverbs and see the difference. He acted stupidly, He acted like an idiot. This is the difference between actions and labels. Actions are temporary and labels are permanent.

Avoid distorted thinking like; **Overgeneralisation.** For one wrong event you make it general, this is overgeneralisation. Failing a test in mathematics, makes me a bad mathematics student. **Personalization.** When things have nothing to do with us but in our imagination would be directed at us. She did not turn up for the meeting because she was sick, and he believes that the reason she did not turn up is because she does not like him. **False conclusions**. By basing the conclusion of an isolated events fails the test, I will fail the whole subject. Or by basing the conclusion on no event at all, failing one subject and I will fail the whole course. **Exaggeration and magnification** This is the process where minor events are seen as major importance. She forgets his birthday and he accuses her of not loving him. Obviously he does not understand what love is. **Polarized thinking** It is a tendency to ignore the middle **ground,** things are either black or white, not grey. The compromise is discarded and the debate does not take place. **Avoid comparisons** We obtain useful information through comparisons. But when it becomes a habit and involves evaluations they are unnecessary. Our old friend the self-esteem, is the culprit again and is too low. It was not as good as the last time. It was not as good as George. There should be individual satisfactions following the performance and accurate assessment of the performance. This comparison stays in the way of the full understanding of one's own capabilities. You cannot be as good as 'X' because you are different, you have different life experiences, different opportunities, different upbringing and you should be as good as you.

In another simplistic way at looking at distorted thinking as comparisons, that you always compare your ego with another ego, the opinions of other people to your performance.

Like comparing Segovia with BB King, they are both masters, who is to say that one is better than the other one? Working on distorted thinking and false comparisons and trigger thoughts we can now work on other problems. The following terms are used such as anger, lack of assertiveness, inability to be open, selfishness, difficulty in accepting others.

Selfishness

Selfishness this is my top of the parade of problem. The trigger thoughts associated with selfishness are: 'I must hang on to what is mine',' Other people do not give anything to me',' If I give things I will regret it afterwards', 'Giving involves losing never living', 'If someone has less than me it is their fault', 'If everybody works as hard as me, they would not need anything from me'. Such a life does not contain the understanding that giving has its own rewards. That the more you give the more there is to go around. Some people are low on their luck. People are not equal at birth in terms of opportunities, and teaching, to base their lives.

Difficulty in accepting others.

Why others are not like I want them to be. This is the main topic of people who have difficulty in accepting others. Nobody has the right to dictate to others what they should think and feel. If everybody wanted people to be the same, it would be boring and also a recipe for disaster.

Inability to open.

These four problems, lack of assertion, inability to open, selfishness, difficulty in accepting others are part of the social intelligence, one of the most important intelligence, your ability to get on well with others, your ability to blend with others. As mentioned before, 85% of success comes from happy involvement with other people. People who do not open up about themselves have the following trigger thoughts:' No one is interested in hearing about me', 'Telling other people my real thoughts give them power over me'. 'If people knew what I am really like I will lose their friendship', For some showing your feelings is a sign of weakness.

Lack of assertion

Trigger thoughts of people who lack in assertion are: 'I will make him angry with me',' I shall look silly', 'I will always end up tongue tied if I try to speak up for my self'. These trigger thoughts arise from early childhood we have rights to stand up for ourselves. That we must do what they like without answering back. The inner rules needs to be replaced by a more appropriate ones. Standing up for your rights is good for everybody. We shall be weary of over assertive people. By asserting ourselves, bit by bit, we will manage to fully assert ourselves. **Anger** like fear it was put there by mother nature. In order to assert yourself over people who trample over you. It was put there to stand up for our rights, or to tell people they crossed the boundary. Anger is an expression of fear, of anxiety. In today's society anger is not accepted e.g. angry with your boss, angry with your parents. Anger poison the system and needs to be taken out. Anger is associated with fight and fear with flight. What gives rise to anger is a threat which can be real or imaginary. Threats can be to our authority, property, security, and so on. Anger, when used verbally can have an effect on relationships, it can upset people, he/she can discard the respect etc. Anger depends on the habit of blaming. As I said, anger poisons the system, and we need to deal with this. With your kicks you can get rid of anger, with shout you can express your anger, with your hands you can kick, and with your teeth you can bite. This is how you deal with anger which cannot be expressed due to society's requirements. Some trigger thoughts of anger are:' How dare she/he says that to me', 'How dare she is trying to get what is mine'. 'How dare you do that I am going to get you.' The best way to deal with anger is to recognize the distorted inner thinking and regulations which give rise to anger and to work on trigger thoughts. Self-control is something else you can use. You are entitled to anger with your boss, but you cannot express it, you need a frustration bag. So you will need to work with anger. Stress that is externally oriented that forces you to do something, that is not good. But stress which is goal oriented is positive and gives you vitality.

Confronting

In order to change you need desire. How badly do you want it. But to change things you need to face them. For any change you will pay the price, the later the change the bigger the price. This is the philosophy of reality, to change yourself where ever you are at the moment. Confronting is healthier than evasion.

Relationships

The most important relationship in your life is the relationship with your parents. It outlasts businesses, careers, marriages. It lasts until passing away. How to grow happy, vibrant, healthy, and loving kids? That comes down to the most important aspects of growing kids and this is self-esteem in children. The role of parents is to generate self-esteem in children. If you do not do that you will fail in your parenthood. You will need to make self-responsible and self-reliant children, who will make other people life's wonderful. They will also make a contribution in their life. They will handle whatever life throws at them. Parents make mistakes, they are allowed to make mistakes, but the main principle in growing children is to give self-esteem to children. They do not belong to us, they are not here to possess, they are here to be nurtured. Principles you need to use when growing children: Do not use destructive criticism. It passes straight into the subconscious mind becoming the truth.

Children need love. You show children your life by looking in the eyes and say 'I love you no matter what you do. I love you unconditionally'. The children need to know the word of love.

Parents are like Gods to children. And children need approval and love in order to grow. Parents need to be supportive, loving and kind. Children need gentleness and praise. Tell them you love them every day, so they know they are loved. If you do not know how to love they will teach you. Things you need to teach children:

Love them unconditionally whatever they do, love them
Eye contact to show your love
Hug and embrace the child as physical contact.
Focus attention on your child. Spend time every day with your child and tell them they are valuable. Believe in your child and tell him that. Allow the valued opinion of your child

Teach the children to love themselves and say over and over 'I like myself', in front of the mirror. Children grown this way are popular, they get along very well with others and have better grades. To grow children you will need to get the ego out of the way. It is possible to apologize to your children to undo the past. Children who have been apologised to by their parents will be transformed overnight. Apologise to your children for the destructive criticism used throughout their lives. Promise not to do it again and allow them to remind you if you use it. 'Is this destructive criticism '? and say 'yes I apologise'.

I have come from a destructive negative environment and hope that this chapter will help people in growing wonderful children.

Mature relationship in the family.

While growing up the parents are the main social context for our lives. Reaching the age of a teenager, the siblings take over this social relationship and do not love their parents too much. Once you reach the age of maturity the relationship with parents comes back and in its place a mature relationship take place. The family, parents and siblings together with children and partners provides the support to grow emotionally and psychologically. As previously said the relationship between you and your parents is a mature relationship and it has the following attributes; **Understanding** As a personal opinion the parents are here to nurture and support even in advanced years. So a sense of understanding of what are we doing by them is important. Otherwise we will change our career and relationship towards something they like. **Space** means freedom from your parents. It means that your parents do not try to interfere with your life. It also means they are not trying to live their lives through you. **Equality** The game of dominance does not have a place in equality. Equality is like a partnership, Parents are not parents anymore, they are your equal. **Support** Means parents will support and help when you need without too much questioning. **Guilt** A constant punishment that we have done something wrong. Guilt is used by parents to control us while growing up. But it can be used also at later stages in lives. If you have done something to feel guilty about then deal with it by atoning or asking God for forgiveness. But when parents are trying to make you feel guilty go on and refuse to give in to guilt. **Love** The expression of love even in maturity is beneficial to both sides. While we grew up with the withdrawal of love, it should not be so in the later stage of the relationship. **Health and strength** A parent with low health and strength will affect us in our relationship with them, no matter how much we want to help. If they give away the control in what should be done to them, this will help and make the situation more bearable, because we will have some control over our lives **Enjoyment** In our teenage years our parents no longer provide us with joy and fulfilment. The pears take the place. This process is part of the growing process where we do not love our parents that much. As previously mentioned this growing up relation is replaced by a more mature one. I know that in these times the parents use guilt to control us and put us down. Maybe it is a sign of not being very close to them. **Acceptance** Also at this moment I do not depend on my parents' approval of me, except for years ago when I was dependent on them. Many people are still depending on the opinion of their parents about them, that they have to prove themselves to their parents, that his mum has an image of the manhood that the son needs to be, that the father has an image of what kind of women his daughter needs to be. **Openness** Open means that you can be honest with your parents about everything. You can refuse, you can disagree with them. The degree of security you enjoy in your relationship is how open you can be with them. If you are not open, you might not be accepted by them and they will withdraw their love from you.

More on Relationships

I would like to spend a little time on relationships because apart from the moment, this is the most abundant thing in life. I would also use relationships as the basis of your emotional life. Major problems in relationships is compatibility. You and the other person is not compatible. It happens more when you are in your twenties. There is nobody at fault it just happens. If Incompatibility will happen you need to move on and look for someone else more compatible on your road in finding your ideal person. Despite incompatibility people still stay in relationships. They do that because of what other people might think about them. You are the person who cares most about your relationship. Relationships are successful if: similarly attracts in all areas sex, money, children, spare time, opposites attract in the areas of temperament. An extrovert is compatible with an introvert person. A 50% extrovert is compatible with a 50% introvert. So, there is no clash in the time the two people talk. Commitment: 100% commitment is required. You do not get out of the relationship. Similarly happy people attract. Do not enter in a relationship where someone is unhappy believing that you can change the other person. People do not change until they follow some things from this book. Liking and respect: is required in a relationship. Infatuation is not enough to keep relationships alive. Communication: You need communication, back and forward. Without communication a relationship dies. You need quantity and quality of communication. Also speaking and listening. Why relationships do not work: Trying to change the other person. As I mentioned before what you see is what you get. People do not change unless they do some of the things from this book. Jealousy nothing to do with the other person but to do with you, you do not feel you are lovable. Say over and over again 'I am a loving, lovable and loved human being'. 'I like myself unconditionally', 'I love myself'. Self-pity, feeling sorry about yourself that you cannot cope say 'I can cope' and get busy. Lack of commitment you only commit yourself as much as the other person does. It is a trading relationship, you need to be fully committed. Amongst other things life is a journey, a journey where you can find the compatible person in your life. Isn't good that that relationships did not work? because I could not find this one. If you want to shorten the waiting time for an ideal relationship you will need to write on a piece of paper, a left column with the good points of the person you want to get and a right column of the bad points of the other person you do not want to have. You will find the person with good points but they will have bad points as well. After this go and find him or her at the appropriate places. Do not go to the pub on Monday because you will not find anything, You will need to make a list of appropriate places. See also what you need in yourself to be able to meet the right person. You can not expect the other person to have all the good points in the world and just a few.

Time management;

If you want to be successful you need to manage your time right. Most of the successful people manage their time right. 80% of results achieved are achieved by the top 20% of people, and that is because they manage their time right. Time management is the direction and control of the events in an effective and efficient way. Make a list of all the things you want to do and then prioritise.

A must be done
B should be done
C could be done (not important)
D delegate
E eliminate

You will also need to focus on clear specific goals in order to achieve them.

Goal settings:

There are thousands of books on goal settings and that is why I am not going to talk to you about goal achievement. Goals need to be your own, not some ones else. You cannot have some ones else goals that goal is for him/her. The goals need to be balanced, you cannot have goals which are about money only or personal development. Goals give you direction, a direction chosen by you. You will be a like a death fish in the water if you do not have goals. Why do you want the goal? this is more important than the goal. The goal can change the reason, stays the same. Make the written goals clear and specific e.g.: I increase my salary by 10 000 at the end of financial year not I have more money. Only have 4 goals at the most. Everything more than that will send you in an anxiety attack. Not less then two goals the thinking will block the superconscious mind from getting through. Stay focused on the goal until you will achieve it. Be open minded. Ask, what if I do more of this? what if I do less of this,? what if I do not do it at all? Use logic and analytical thinking to solve the problem, and if you cannot solve it, give it to the superconscious mind and get on with other problems. The above process is called acting intelligently which you can do even if you did not go to university. I urge to master it and use it all the time. The goal will meet you on your path to the goal. Also dwell on the goal and feel like you have it already. It will attract your goal faster. The goals need to match your values otherwise you will not feel satisfactions.

Human capacity to develop.

Constructive attitudes when you take a constructive view and approach to life, to relationships, to work, to personal development etc. Most of the success is attitudinal from constructive attitudes. Self-concept is the bundle of beliefs, the master programme to your computer. Self-concept is made of self-esteem, self-ideal and self-image. Self-esteem is how you feel about yourself. To increase your self-esteem you say over and over "I like myself more today than yesterday, and I like myself more tomorrow than today'. The self esteem is measured by how much you love yourself how much you like yourself. Children come into this world with 'full potential'. They are spontaneous, are unafraid and uninhibited. When you achieve greatness you will be uninhibited and unafraid. To control their children parents use destructive criticism. Instead of controlling their children, constructive criticism develops two negative habits which create fear of failure and fear of rejection. Fear of failure leads to failure in life. Fear of rejection leads to conditional love. 'If you do not, you are going to get it', You are not loved until you do what we want you to do. Both these fears are destructive to life. Self esteem is my favourite topic in personal development. And I think it will eventually be adopted by the whole world. Let's say in 100 years. Self-esteem is the core to your self-concept.

Catharsis and suppressed emotions:

Catharsis is the re-experience of a traumatic event and expressing strong emotions associated with them. It is a safe expression of emotions. When I left the communist system for a capitalist one I had a traumatic experience. I used catharsis for this event and found a new way of thinking of the event and after the event. As you increase your self-esteem it will become easier and easier to get into event. The catharsis experiment will unblock your emotions and will allow new flow of energy. It will also allow you to look at the event with a different more healthy view. Expressing your emotions is a healthy way, but sometimes is not socially acceptable. You cannot get upset with your boss, you cannot get steam off at the soccer ground. To find a place to do it is very important. Women and men with unexpressed emotions are more vulnerable to depression and anxiety, during their lifetime. These people are also left with blockage of energy required for running their life. The key in dealing with repressed emotion is to accept them for what they are, emotions and energy. By accepting the feeling we feel at ease because there is no resistance. So a much better way is too observe them rather than resist them. There is a limit of energy let out by emotions. Be calm and relaxed, eventually the pressure will run out and so do the repressed emotions. Another way in dealing with suppressed emotions is to express them in an accepting way. You can play an instrument which can be started at any age with one hour of play a day. I personally use the electric guitar I started playing at age of 19; too late to play in a band, that was my belief. Anyway to have a successful band you require a lot of effort and energy. There are millions of guitars player in the world. Whenever I feel lonely or need to release some of the unexpressed emotions, I use the guitar. You can also paint if you like that, and it can be started at any age. You can go to the gym and do various sports if you are in a good shape. To express feelings of love you can always have a dog as a pet. Dogs are very good, but keep in mind they need attention and affection. You will get a lot of love in return. Personally, I prefer cats, because I do not have the time and energy and place to grow a dog.

Getting around the right people

It is not the people who help you but the right people you surround yourself with, that help you. Letting the right people on the bus is vital to your success. And this is regardless of where you are going. You will need to appreciate them and not be put off by the boredoms of the relationship. I had nice people, mirror people like me but never appreciated them and

I lost them. Finding and keeping the right people is a vital step in your life. I hope you learn from me and do not repeat my mistakes. These right people will help you, protect from society which has a negative influence, like a wall of positive energy. It is very important to know that you are isolated by society's negative influences. By the power of suggestion you will get the colour of your environment. People who are positive, people who want to go somewhere, people who have goals and ideals like you. It is not going to be an easy task to find them, trust me I have been looking for a while. If you find him or her keep them, they are hard to find.

In your life there are 3 categories of people. People who are close to you and very influential. You spend a lot of time with them. People who you see once a week for a coffee with some level of influence. People who you meet once a month who do not influence you. People who you admire through magazines, brochures and publications, who also have an influence on you, by the power of suggestion. Even if you only see them in the magazines.

Social Intelligence.

I have covered so far relationships, intimate relationships and loving relationships. They are all part of the social intelligence package. Your ability to blend and get on with people. Social intelligence is the most important intelligence, since only by being with people you will achieve satisfactions and fulfilment in life, 85% of success is achieved with people. You will get kicked out of a few places and then you realize how good it is to get on well with others.

All my life I have had problems with people and is fair to say that only these days I get on well with people. My friendly nature has brought me to these days. Even if I feel good with people, the game of numbers is not for me. Since you could not go further in life, I needed to learn the game of numbers. This game of numbers was probably developed thousands of years ago, I hate. Everybody sounds the same. Everybody has the same answers. Even the assertiveness of people is the same, or better said, there are only a finite number of models of assertiveness. With the word 'sorry' I always crack a joke so not to sound the same, regardless of people's age. Despite me not liking the game you will need to learn it, to know it well. It is very important in your ability to get on well with others. If you land in a group do not be the first or the last one, be in the middle that is the best policy and save you a lot of energy.

Also, very important is to assert yours self, make sure you assert yourself. Also, you may have a hard time doing it, but you need to do it. Until the age of 35 I did not do any assertiveness, I was living in my own world, withdrawn and shy. Make sure you know the people in the position of power, just to know how to deal with the situation. You also do not want to annoy them. The way on getting along with people is by the game of numbers. In a group of people, as soon as you meet them, stay back and let others do the talk. Until you find what they are really about and then integrate in the group. Be aware of people some are more external like Australians, some are more internal like me, and some are more balanced between external and internal. Your self-esteem will enhance your ability to get on well with others (with self-esteem the less you fear anything). Enhancing someone else self-esteem will increase yours as well e.g.: 'you put so much effort into your job'. The compliment should be sincere and done immediately. If you are not sincere, people would pick up and that would not be a compliment. Practice some replies for yourself during the day. They will become very handy. Some people would practice in front of television. Be assertive and you get plenty of respect and they will let you stay there in their place. A nice and easy way of practising social skills is to have a group of people you meet every day of the week on different days. That will make you practice social skills Also you should get a job in which you will get your social skills.

Something which I wanted to say is not to lose yourself in the game of numbers just because you practice it every day. After all it is only a game. And the more you accept it as a game, the better your life. Something you need to know is to hold your own, this is the ultimate goal in social intelligence.

Financial freedom and financial abundance.

You need financial freedom so you do not get pushed around by the government and you have enough money to be free. You do not rely on the government money. I put this chapter at the end of the book because if you are not happy you will not enjoy the financial freedom. So there is a requirement in the development stage. It is believed that more than a hundred thousand dollars will not make any difference on the happiness scale.

Some people are not interested in money, money does not make any difference to them. The truth is that money matters. You will need to buy food, health, books, trips and in general the good things in life. So, we perceive the financial freedom to be important. Another truth is that you see people with a lot of money not being happy or just happy a little bit. Or if they are running out of money they get back to being unhappy. And it is a good thing because if you do not have money you can still be happy.

You need to know why you want financial freedom. You need to know what you need in order to have financial abundance. What contributions do you want to make in terms of finance. Personally financial freedom is not enough for me. It will not do it. I have high standards in terms of the house I want, the car I want, the holiday I want etc. Financial freedom will not do it. Earning 50 000$ a year will not do it. In the end I will probably rely on government money. To help people as well I need 100 million. 90 million for people who are entrepreneurs and need money to start new business. The money will be given as long as they have a good business proposition. For me there will be 10 million for the house and other expenses. This is what I want, who knows? I might end up on the government pensions, but financial freedom will not do it. In Australia we save money 10% of the salary, compulsive in superannuation companies who invest the money. This money may be used at later stage in life in retirement to supplement the government pensions. In The Richest Man in Babylon by George Clayson, which I read years ago, they are talking about compounding where you put money into an account without you touching the money. He mentioned 10% to save and 10% to give away. In the beginning money grows slowly, but what happens when it gets a momentum? The money will increase exponentially. This is good for younger people but what happens when you are older? You will need to become an investor or keep working until you die, 3 to 4 days a week. A good way to invest is in stock. In the stock market you do not lose money until you sell. People buy at low prices and sell at high prices. That is if the stock broker wants to buy the stock you recommend. The stock market is complicated especially in the area of puts, calls, options derivatives in general. Until they will make it simpler you will need qualifications in trading from the TAFE courses. Once you have this you will be able to trade every morning on computers without the need of a stock broker. You will learn mathematics and economics required to apply various financial systems. After 2 years of practice you will become an investor. This is one hour a day in the morning. I had the goal of trading a long time ago, but it never materialized. Maybe one day I will do it. I will do it because I have a good knowledge in mathematics. When you are young you can lose money and start over again. When you are older it is harder to start again money. What you will give away will come back, this is Karma. Be an investor but also give away money. One way to make money is to sell books, lots of them. A lot of people do that and become rich over nigh, although is a hard way to make money because there are millions of books being published. By the way, I do not know where my money will come from.

And finally to have financial abundance you will need to spend less then you earn and invest the rest.

You will need to:

Define what you want in terms of money,
Design an achievable plan to follow
Be fully responsible, do not give away responsibility.
When it is tough keep going
Get a coach to help you

Relaxation

There are so many books on relaxation so I will not make a big deal about it. Current mindfulness is the meditation taken by a lot of people. It is a meditation in which you live for the moment. You will not have time for fear, because in the present there is no fear. I do it myself and is very good, that is the reason I added it to this book. Focus on the places of the body in the moment. Eg.my back lies on my bed, my head rests on the pillow. Also be aware of your environment the corner of the furniture is there, the bed seats on the floor etc. I hope you get the logic here. If you find yourself drifting, do not get upset, just go back to meditation and watch how you drifted. Another type of meditation I use is transcendental meditation. Align the body, mind and brain to work together. It is very good for relaxation. Focus on your breathing. Out or in or both kinds of breathing. The mind will wonder and you need to observe it and go back to meditation. Say' there is a thought' or 'there is an emotion.' With practice you will become good and you will be able to do short bursts meditation for 15 seconds. That is all it will take you to relax. Another type of meditation I use is tape affirmations with music. It relaxes the mind body and brain. So the affirmations will be accepted very easily. With music in the background you can count from zero to twenty. Then you will get into a deep state of relaxation where you can listen to your affirmations. You can put anything on affirmations, gaining self esteem would be a good one. Energy is another good one. There are more types of relaxation which you will find if you look for them.

The Process of Death

This subject can be easily placed after acquiring self-esteem, but I decided to put it last. Once you acquire self esteem you will be able to go anywhere and cover various situations in your life. On the scale of development the process of death comes after the acquisition of self esteem. Before you live, you need to die, before you die you need to live. So much truth in this statement taken from the bible. As is believed by many, the process of death is not about stopping to exist biologically. It is about living your life. What is that you want from life.? If by any chance you live your life and get what you want from life you would not fear death. I lived my life. I have done the best I could with the knowledge at the time in my life. I have done what I was sent to do, now I can ascend to the next level. In general there would be something you did not achieve in this life. Again how you deal with this is part of the process of death. A lot of people believe there is no life after death. That there is no higher level. If you think of the reason you were sent here you would realize there is another world. The soul never dies, the spirits exists, and the mind ascents and grows by acquiring total knowledge in this world. Plenty of reasons to believe there is another world. Another factor in the process of death is to believe that you have done your best with the knowledge at the time. It is easier to manage your life, when you think you have done your best. I was a good a father, I was a good worker, I was a good husband, I achieved my mission. Even if you have not achieved your mission, even the fact that you tried is something. The things which could not have been done, will be done in another world. You cannot stay in this world and do things over and over again, that is the comfort zone. There is also a natural emotion called boredom, so you will get bored after a while. To stay in the same relationship in this world would be unthinkable. What you will find in this world is moments and relationships which will not last. Another part of the process of death (or better said the process of life) is aging. Despite whatever opinion you have for yourself aging is a number. There is no difference between a healthy 20 year old and a 60 year individual. They can both do the same, provided they are healthy. The hair become silver in colour and the skin gets wrinkles. Do not equate wrinkles and silver hair with getting old it is not an appropriate definition. The eastern philosophy teachers equate aging with stopping to learn and grow. We are all here, in this world, for others with a mission. Until we change the world we are all here for others. It is a world of pain and that needs to be changed. Probably if you see animals put down at the abattoir so we can eat, you will probably not eat any meat. I know it takes a lot of energy and effort to be a vegetarian and even trees are probably hurting. Animals are not scared if you let them go by themselves to slaughter. It is when they are pushed to do things that makes them uncomfortable. Another reason you should not feel scared about dying is that it only takes place when you fulfil your mission. If you die without fulfilling your mission it is because you died living on the edge, driving formula 1 cars and going in a balloon around the world. In general people who die in the 80's or 90's are people who do not fulfil their mission and did not live on the edge. There can also be missions which take a long time to fulfil, that is why people would live until late in their lives. You should also realize that dying biologically is part of living and it might happen. To recapitulate the process of death is the realisation that you did not live your life here (there is another world). It is easier to believe that there is anther world, in order to deal with life. If you do not live on the edge, or you are not a free spirit (free spirit dies), you will die when you fulfil your mission. Accept your self unconditionally, see yourself as a good father, as good worker etc. Do not believe in aging, it only happens when you stop learning.

CHAPTER III

Miscellaneous

Happiness

Is something that everybody wants no matter what stage of life they are at. The state of being happy is the ultimate goal of human beings and desired by everyone. One way to live your life is with so much joy, happiness and energy that you forget there is a past or a future. At most that is my desire. I might not be able to achieve that but I will pursue it no matter what happens. Happiness is a daily state of your system. It is the feeling of being happy.

Music therapy:

We mentioned in the book that you do affirmations with music. That would balance the brain, the left side with the right side, you will feel calm and tranquil. One way to be calm is through music. If you read a book with music in the background, you will do a lot of reading into a calm state. Relaxation music is part of music therapy. There is also music uplifting and energy for the soul. The music should be without words. Expressing your feelings through an instrument is again music therapy. Music helps you to stay on positive not on negative emotions. The right music can give you rhythm and then you can do a lot of things. There is a lot of material if you want to continue with music therapy.

Social anxiety:

Social anxiety is a fear that you are criticised, evaluated or judged by others. It can become more serious and you will develop social phobia. Shyness can become a social anxiety if it is not unbearable. In shyness we will have a feeling of self consciousness, what would people think about me? Typical trigger thoughts in social anxiety are: 'Hi, he is looking at me', 'He or she thinks I am not worthy', 'Hi, what am I going to do'? (I am getting evaluated). No matter what others may say social anxiety is a form of performance anxiety, where you do not know how to handle the situation, when you do not know what to say, and how to behave. In order to deal with social anxiety you will need to start with one person, practicing your social skills. With a bit of anti anxiety medication such as Paroxetine known as SSRI anti depressants (paroxetine is good because it does not mask the cognitive thinking, it takes the edge off fear) you will be able to handle social situations. The cognitive thoughts associated with social phobias need to be replaced by more helpful ones. If you handle the situation with one person you should be able to handle the situations with many people. We live in a society where performance is seen everyday. A society of 'stars' made by people, 'stars' which perform. If you have been suffering from social anxiety in isolation it will take a while to be sociable with every body. I do not have to talk let the others start and do the talking. Talking is learned. Once I encounter the situation I will be better at it. The main point is to assert your self.

Unfinished business:

Unfinished business is relationship which are finished but you still hang on to them. Relationships with your ex boss, with the member of the opposite sex or even the same sex. You still feel about that person and you are angry and hurt by him/her. You are entitled to anger and hurt by holding on to it. For long times it is not healthy for everybody. You can write a letter and burn it, so you will let go of hurt and anger. It is selfish and appropriate to write a letter. If burning once the letter does not help, try burning it more times. It takes a while getting it out of the system.

Dear X,

I hate you because you hurt me. You hurt me by leaving me out (or any reasons the person did it to you). You hurt me by not talking to me. Despite all these I forgive you and let you go. I forgive you because you are stupid and do not understand that I am a worthy and valuable human being. I am worthy because God says so. In the face of God we are all worthy and valuable human beings. I forgive you and let you go. You are free and I am free. Sign and burn the letter and the anger and hurt should be diminished. Some people say you should write the letter and mail the letter. But you do not want the other person to be involved. Other things that might help is to look at the other person's negative points, this makes it easier to forget.

Free Spirit:

Would you like to be a free spirit? Maybe you do, so enjoy going from one person to others on any social strata. From prostitutes to CEO of companies. You will enjoy their company and also learning from them. Free spirit. The only problem with free spirit is that you will not be able to stay alive. The sooner you get away from the free spirit the better.

Habits:

We are creatures of habit and what we do over and over again becomes a habit. Good healthy habits versus the negative habits which do not help us. Always develop a habit of being positive. Always look for the good in everything. This is good for your mental health. Habits of saving and investing Money are good for your financial situation. The habit of getting up in the morning doing your affirmations and review your goals. Develop as many good habits as you can.

Fights:

Is it fair and healthy to say that we fight amongst ourselves? In a world where life is short is fighting appropriate? Unfortunately even if you stop fighting the fact that the world is fighting, we can not get away from it. It is advisable that you learn how to fight and pick the fights you want or think are appropriate. Do not fight with everybody like some people do. Picking your own fights is the right attitude. There are people who, if they stop fighting do not know what else they can do in their life. Similarly for people who get you, once they have got you and you accept them and they look for a different challenge, in other people. People do not know how to live. This is the ego talking.

Main stream versus supportive stream:

There are two streams in this world. The supportive people who support the main-stream and the supported stream the main-stream of people. Without the supportive stream the main-stream would not exist. The supportive streams builds institutions, organisations, companies, etc. everything which is required for human existence. In Australia 70% of people are the supported, and 30% are the supportive, this is because there are migrants involved in the building of the country. In the world in general the ratio is 35% to 65%. The main stream of people make a living are pumping up their ego and scared about loosing their lives. Some of the people in the stream are mixing with each other. You need to know how to deal with each stream. Of particular interest are the unidimensional, people who will only have one dimension and do things because they have to. Some of them are simpleton, they see things simple even if they are not. They will enter the supportive stream to get dimensions from those.

Dwell on what you want:

If you dwell on what you want you will not have time for fear. And by attractions you will achieve your goal. One emotion will dominate the other emotions so keep to the positive ones.

Take your opportunities:

If you are a great man, a lot of life time opportunities will be facing you. Picking ones which are right for you and letting go off others is the challenge for you. The ones right for you means those which match your passion and what you could become the best in the world and your economic denominator if you have one. The more dimension you have the more opportunities you will get. If you are not a great man lifetime opportunities and opportunities in general should be taken. It will make life easier and give you new directions. If you have more dimensions you will work better with the superconscious mind and God.

Visualization:

Despite what many people would say, visualization is not good for your life, particularly if you are prone to anxiety. The brain will give you unhappy pictures and you will need to shake your head to get rid of them. They will also block your superconscious solutions. Instead of visualization , imagining the feeling will have a better effect.

Attitude:

85% of success is attitudinal. Constructive attitude is a way of looking at the situation constructively. There are attitudes which are constructive versus the ones which are destructive. Constructive attitudes towards your work, relationships, personal development, mission, people, life etc. are the key to a positive mental health. Today in society a lot of people are destructive and they look to put not much in the system but to get a lot which of course does not work.

Good leaders:

I brought up this chapter about enduring great leaders because they are not many. However, the more they are the bigger the contribution to changing the world and the better for the human race. I have to admit that great leaders are probably born that way. I am not an expert in leadership, I want to make a point about great leaders. Some of the qualities of good leaders are: commitment and passion, good communication, decision making capabilities, creativity and innovativeness, accountability, delegation and empowerment, confidence, honest and integrity. He or she needs to inspire others and need to have empathy. According to Jim Collins in his book 'From good to great', he or she will need to be also an effective leader, a competent manager, a contributing team member and a highly capable individual. Not in this order but all the qualities need to be explored. He needs to be humble and fearless/ modest and wilful.

Seriousness

Do not take your life too seriously, loosen up. We mentioned in the book that you change embarrass to amuse, and it is so true. The only thing serious is 'control' and life. Life is not a rehearsal, this is it. But taking things too seriously, being hard on yourself is not the way to go. You are more successful if you see the fun out of the situation. Also amuse yourself. What is better to amuse yourself than human stupidity. Human stupidity was put into this world at birth. So, this is how you were meant to be. Amusing yourself every day. Einstein once said: 'Human stupidity and space are infinite but I do not know about space'. It is so true. But as I said it is an instrument with which you have fun every day. Until we learned we are all stupid. So, you also need to face your stupidity and at the same time learn. If by any chance you are suffering of CFS 'standard' you can use the affirmations given to you in the book and be happy. At least for a couple of hours, after you wake up. Affirmations said before you go to bed, are then picked up by the hypnopompic state. You have enough information to be happy for some time. Some people would say, go to the supermarket and slap somebody on the bottom. This is to take you out of the comfort zone so, you get a bit of fear. Do not fear anything because the people are not going to do anything to you. What I also recommend, and you will be able to do it, when you go home and are by yourself rehearse your good time moments so this will double your moments in the day. In this way you are multiplying your good moments. Usually people rehearse the bad times so fear is taking time. We change this to the positive experiences. I used this technique myself for a long time, and for some reasons dropped it. It is no longer in my repertoire. So, I consider this as a fact of life. Since the supreme goal of human beings is to be happy, I hope you will apply it to you. There are people who say you cannot be happy until you get rid of ignorance. It is not true, you can be happy and ignorant, you are on your way to lose your ignorance.

Falling asleep.

We assume that you do not have any problems with sleep despite, the fact that 50% of the population has a sleeping problem. If you cannot fall asleep you can read a book. In many cases this helps. If you say to yourself aloud "I lay down in bed and fall sleep' just as you get into bed and try to fall a sleep you will sleep. I have done this for years and this has worked with no problems.

Support Group

If have done everything and you are comfortable with the level of development you have achieved, but things do not go well, you will probably need support. Support groups about which these books are, will help you a lot. You are on your road to full potential with lots of dimensions. The more dimensions you have the more likely you are to work with the superconscious mind and God. Working with the superconscious mind and God will be easily done because you are complete. At the support group you will need to find the person with which you connect. The person who will be there for you and the person who will be there for themselves. If by any chance you do not find him/her keep trying. Do the shopping until you find the right merchandise, until you find the right person.

Confidence

One important part of you is believing in yourself. Being confident in any interactions in your life. An important aspect is social confidence. As previously discussed social intelligence is the most important intelligence, meaning you put as number one confidence, social intelligence confidence. The idea does not mean that other confidences do not matter. One way to acquire confidence is to repeat the event over and over again whatever you are doing until you reach one level of confidence. Another way to acquire confidence is through the superconscious mind. And this is a faster way in achieving an overall confidence. Think about how important you are, the a center you are, how you can do anything with confidence. At any time you do not expect the confidence to come to you from the superconscious mind like a detonator, it will come. You will need to take actions immediately so the superconscious mind believes that you are serious. Now I have not seen this written anywhere but I proceed with this and acquire confidence myself. So is a proven method of acquiring confidence, if it does not work with you, it means that you have to acquire it in a different way. Almost always I use the grated teeth approach where I use anger in accomplishing confidence. I say it with confidence 'can't I fucking do this' and proceed to do it with confidence from anger. By repeating over and over again you will become a master at what you are doing. Which ever way you accomplish confidence is good for you. If you do not believe in yourself, you will never achieve anything. To say the opposite 'I can't do it', it robs you from achieving anything in your life. Before doing anything, you should believe in yourself. You should not follow what people tell you. If the goal you have is important, people will put you down, they will give you reasons why is not achievable. Unless he or she is a very important friend do not tell anybody about your goals. They feel insecure because they do not have goals. Whenever you doubt yourself achieving something, that is a sign of no confidence Look to God to tell you the reasons you will succeed. Have trust in God who wants you to do well and he loves you too.

Changing the world

Give me a button to change the world and I would probably be the first one to press it. (I think there are a lot of people who would like to change the world straight away). Can we easily change the world? No, I do not think so. You can make a significant contribution or be a model, a lot of people would mould themselves. Can we have a movement that will change the world? No. These had been tried prematurely with negative results. Jesus after 2000 years has 2.3 billion followers out of 7.53 billion. Also Buddha has 535 million followers and Muhammad has 1.2 billion followers. Their contribution is significant and the message of universal love is thoroughly spread, but the world has not changed. There is hurt wherever you go. The world will eventually change but not yet. There are at least 200 years until we change the world so there is no hurt. Most of the knowledge to do that is currently acquired. Actually, a lot of discoveries were done 2000 years ago. A lot of people would say that all the discoveries are done and there is nothing new to discover. I disagree as there is always something to discover, even though most of the knowledge has been found.

Say nice things to people

If you do not have anything nice to say to people do not say anything. This is what goes around in society today. Well is not quite like that. This is a simplistic interaction with people. As you know 85% of success comes from happy interaction with people. What you say comes back to you in waves. Words have power and this is true for the person receiving it and the person who uses it. People have a nice sign, saying 'say something nice to me, something beautiful'. Words of inclusion rather than words of separation, words of acceptance rather than rejection, words of love rather then words of hate, words of praise rather than words of criticism, works

If you express words of appreciation, words of appreciation will come back to you. If you express gratitude, gratitude will come back to you. If you express arrogance and rudeness that is what will come back to you.

When you say something nice about people be prompt say straight away. I remember once saying nice things about the British people, that they are 'polite, articulate and also funny' to a British Lady. At later stages when I was fighting with an acquaintance she took my side and protected me and fought for me. Another time I said nice things about a doctor and she took my side in many situations. In general, people of a low level of education, after they assert themselves use problem talking and then gossiping and because of their negative effect this two should not be used. You talk about problem you attract the problem, you talk about gossip you will jump to wrong conclusions it is better that you come to your own conclusions. Gossiping is good for social intelligence. Types of personality are uncovered.

In relation to people, winning their heart should be your goal, superior to the game of numbers. It is also a higher level of relationship, a superior attitude.

Completeness

Have you ever wondered what you will do if you are not married. You are by yourself left on the shelves, as it is known. Is this the end of the world? Despite so much knowledge acquired in this world there are so many things to do until we change the world. So here we go there are so many things to do with your life. There is no doubt that the world needs to be changed, and we can do that together. But until you change it, we need to do more things, to be more and to have more as well, and achieve your potential by fulfilling your mission, also known as a calling. Everybody has the potential of numerous dimensions and a lot of siblings including mine have only one dimension. And that is the game of numbers, one dimension of which, if you do not have it, you will have a hard time in your life. I know this first hand because I left it last in my development, not liking it very much. I managed to live my life with a lot of friends. The game of numbers is found everywhere you go, and is not something I am impressed by. There are a lot of dimensions and if you add them to yourself and try to be complete, you will travel better with the superconscious mind, as well as with God. So, when you ask from the superconscious or God, things will come easier to you because you are complete. So, one way to travel in this world is to add dimensions to your personal development. Dimensions such growing a child, developing healthy intimate relationships, social intelligence, acquiring self esteem and others should be your aim, and these can be used instead of getting married, taught by Christian religions. So do not worry that you are not married because you can develop yourself by adding more dimension and live an easier life because you can travel with the superconscious mind.

Conclusion

It is believed that schizophrenia is a life time condition where there is no cure, that you will have to find a 'balance' in your system to live like other people live. This is with a concept about it where there are times of well being and times of hallucinations and delusions. The less delusions you have the better the condition, I knew 20 years ago how to cure schizophrenia and it was to my disbelief to hear that there is no cure that you have to live all your life with it.

It is believed that there are approximately 250 000 people with schizophrenia in Australia. Personally I dispute this number which says

1 % of population has schizophrenia. I do not know how they came to such a conclusion. I am not an authority in the condition and do not have a great knowledge about it, I had to research and see what type of schizophrenia there are. Factors which influence the rise of schizophrenia and other things were research. I know you only need to live with the condition for 2 to 3 years and the condition is not an insecurity but a functional condition. The world is not a perfect place. Things go wrong for example, dying in a air balloon journey because you live on the edge and even if you did not fulfill your mission you can die because it is not a perfect world. It happens when you live on the edge. So, my contribution to schizophrenia is the cure of the condition. From now on there should not be any life time sentencing to schizophrenia but 2 to 3 years for the fragment to be taken over by the new bigger fragment. It is also a privilege to achieve your mission by fulfilling yourself by empowering yourself. So, I am not an authority in schizophrenia like I am in addiction and chronic fatigue syndrome but I am a guy who wants to make a contribution to schizophrenia and that is how to get well. See it as a temporary part of your life. I was diagnosed myself with schizophrenia but it is only the disorganized type, where energy at the level of the mind is not there to follow. At the right time this is easily fixed. So, I hope I have achieved the purpose of the book.